TIA CHUCHA PRESS
CHICAGO

## Acknowledgments

A special thanks to R.R. Donnelly & Sons Company for the underwriting of *I Represent: A Collection of Literary Works from Gallery 37* and the Chicago Community Trust for underwriting the 1995 literary programs at Gallery 37.

A special thanks also goes to Peggy Fiedler, Gallery 37 Development Coordinator, for her hard work and dedication in seeing this project through to completion.

Gallery 37 is a program of the Chicago Department of Cultural Affairs with private funding made possible through the Arts Matter Foundation, a 501(c)3 organization.

The work in this volume was gathered from Gallery 37 participants in Summer 1995.

Printed in the United States of America.

ISBN 0-938903-21-7

BOOK DESIGN: Jane Brunette
COVER ART: Robert Glover, age 15; Ebony Silas, age 15;
Fred Green, age 17; Megan Iwamuro, age 15
PART OPEN ART: Part 1—Alfonso Santoyo, age 19; Part 2—Megan Vandehey, age 19;
Part 3—Megan Vandehey, age 19; Part 4—Justis Roe, age 19

PUBLISHED BY:
TIA CHUCHA PRESS
*A Project of the Guild Complex*
PO Box 476969
Chicago IL 60647

*Tia Chucha Press is partially supported by the National Endowment for the Arts, the Illinois Arts Council and the Lannan Foundation.*

# ABOUT GALLERY 37

As Chicago's award-winning arts education program that provides Chicago
youth, ages 14 to 21, with job training in the arts, Gallery 37 is an international model which demonstrates that the arts offer an exciting and feasible
framework for teaching basic work skills. Started in 1991, this program was
designed to provide innovative summer employment and arts education to
Chicago high school students, and to increase public awareness of the arts as a
tool for learning, critical thinking, building self-esteem and molding career
choices. Gallery 37 has brilliantly captured the imagination of young people
throughout the city, transforming the Loop, neighborhoods, parks, youth
centers and schools into workshops of artistic discovery and meaningful
employment in the literary and visual arts. Since it's inception in 1991,
Gallery 37 has employed over 3,500 apprentice artists in the Downtown,
Neighborhood and Chicago Public Schools' After School programs, and has
employed over 550 professional artists.

*Gallery 37 Committee*
Maggie Daley, Chair

*Gallery 37 Director*
Cheryl Hughes

*City of Chicago*
Richard M. Daley, Mayor

*Department of Cultural Affairs*
Lois Weisberg, Commissioner

The following organizations are literary participants in Gallery 37 activities:

## YOUNG CHICAGO AUTHORS

*Bob Boone, Executive Director*

In 1992, as outgrowth of his work with young people in Chicago, Bob Boone established Young Chicago Authors. This program has several components. The workshops concentrate on helping groups of young people discover their writing talent. The writing scholars program is directed at different populations, but they rest upon the same assumptions:

> —All young people, including young people from the inner-city, can write well.

> —One of the biggest obstacles to successful writing is a lack of confidence.

> —Creative writing is a proven technique for helping young people acquire confidence in writing.

> —Success in creative writing can lead to success with other forms of writing.

> —Success in writing can lead to success in school.

> —Success in writing can lead to professional success.

> —Success in writing can lead to personal satisfaction.

## PEGASUS PLAYERS

*Arlene Crewdson, Executive Director*

Pegasus Players is the oldest cultural institution in Chicago's Uptown neighborhood, one of the most economically diverse communities in the city. While offering an award-winning season of plays to the general public, Pegasus has a deep commitment to audiences who have little access to the arts. In fact, Pegasus is one of the major providers of arts programs to the inner-city young people of Chicago through the Chicago Young Playwrights Festival program. Over 37,000 Chicago teenagers have benefited from the Festival since its inception ten years ago. This arts education program and writing contest for Chicago teenagers culminates with the original winning one-act plays enjoying a professional production as part of Pegasus' mainstage season. It is a program that involves teaching teachers to use play writing techniques as a continuing education tool to facilitate critical thinking and self esteem.

The Young Playwrights Festival has expanded to embrace several related initiatives. The theatre has been involved with Gallery 37 for three summers, and last summer, the theatre ran its own play writing program through the city's Community Academy/Mentoring Initiatives Program. Pegasus Players created jobs for over eighty inner-city youths during the summers of '92 and '93 with their unique play writing and arts education programming through the Chicago Initiative Call to Action.

## GUILD COMPLEX

*Michael Warr, Executive Director*

The Guild Complex, an independent, award-winning, not-for-profit cultural center, serves as a forum for literary cross-cultural expression, discussion and education, in combination with other arts. We believe that the arts are instrumental in defining and exploring the human experience, while encouraging participation by artist and audience alike in changing the conditions of our society. Through its culturally inclusive, primarily literary programming, the Guild Complex provides the vital link that connects communities, artists and ideas.

Known for the high quality and diversity of its weekly literary readings and performances by emerging and established writers, the Complex often combines the spoken word with music, dance, video and the visual arts.

Tia Chucha Press, the publishing wing of the Guild Complex, has established an international reputation for books of poetry that effectively combine poetry that matters and superb artistry. By publishing the best of emerging cross-cultural and socially-engaged poets, Tia Chucha Press has played a vital role in keeping alive the literary awakening that has been recently linked to Chicago, a poetry rebirth that has now swept the nation and many parts of the world.

# Contents

# III: DREAMING IN BLUE LIGHTS

# IV: EXCUSES! EXCUSES!

# PREFACE

Chicago.
International flavor with a midwestern aftertaste.
A pot that could use a little more melting.
Mostly, we separate like oil and water.
We are tourists of familiar landscapes.
We have friends from the northside who have never been south
    of Comiskey Park.
We know folks from the southside who haven't experienced anything north
    of the Loop.
And, there are people who know only that west is the opposite direction
    of Lake Michigan.
We have so many cultures represented in this city.
There is much we could learn from one another.
Each block has a million stories.
Every culture possesses a unique form of expression.
From Hip-Hop to Mozart, Monet to Tito Puente.
It is in our stories, our art, that we celebrate our differences and
discover our commonalities.
It is at this place that we learn respect. That we more than understand,
    we overstand.
Gallery 37 is a place like this.
A gathering place.
A coming togetherness.
A neutral zone where 1,200 hungry minds congregate to feed one another.
Not to build walls, but destroy them.
Those who blindly pass the downtown tent village reside in isolation.
Inside, we are creating a world.
We are weaving the future.
It's not peace through fashion, like some Bennetton ad.
It's an honest concern for the  hood, the school, the city these young citizens
are to inherit.
Let these words speak on their behalf.
Morsels of wisdom from those who represent tomorrow.
Now.

*—Quraysh Ali*
*June 1996*

The human spirit is an amaranth;
boasting life and healthiness
Long after the death of its roots.

**ANTHONY ANTONIADIS**

# IMITATING THE SMOKE

1

*Lekeishia S. McGee*

# WHISPERS

We look into the heavens
    for something to separate
our past from our future,
    And reveal what's cloaked
between the stars.
    We turn ears to the wind
listening for whispered messages
    from the time glacier rivers
fed an ocean of ice where
    our houses now
        stand.

We search vaulted faces
    for locked truths,
keys missing, we follow many
            trails.
But the best are those we
make ourselves.

*Jivon Mackey*

## UNTITLED

I roar like a lion
which means I will be heard.
I glow like a flower
in my own little world.
I soar like an eagle
ready to explore.
I'm silent like a tree
when I cannot speak.
These are the images
that describe me.

*Natasha Binion*

# MY WORLD

My world comes to an end
by lacking what it is
I need to survive.
How can I receive what I need
If I don't have the knowledge
or the skills?

If there were no boundaries
I would fly in my mind
to things I cannot find.
I would fly off the end of the world.
Imagine . . .


I am me.
No one could ever copy
or do what I do.
No one could bring peace
to my mind, body, and soul
but me in my own world.

*Jessica Savolainen*

# INNOCENCE

Her young innocence burning
   Away
Falling into a pile of gray ash
   A little girl in her mother's shadow
shall soon realize
   She is a mother in a little girls shoes
Crying into this pile of ash
   She twists and turns like ribbons in
the sky
   Scared to look, but she can't help
Peeking through her fingers
   As she peers into the mirror
Tears run over her fingers and
   shatter on her bare feet
She sees an image of a woman she can't
   bear to be
She cuts away at her life in hopes
   Something
   Anything
Might change
   And as blood runs down her arms and legs
She dances one last dance
   A dance for life
A dance for death
   And she reaches her arms up to the sky
Asking for some salvation
   But, to no avail, she was not answered
So as the incense burned to the end
   She ended her dance with one last twist
Imitating the smoke
   Ending it all with a fall
And on the floor
There she lay

A beautiful little girl
or shall I say
WOMAN
With all her innocence
Burned away
All that was left
was a pile of gray ash

*Susan Kurek*

# WHITE ROSES

A beautiful bird with sad, lonely brown eyes sat in a golden cage.

Her color was a precious snow white and

her innocence was as pure as the heavens.

Chained with desire inside a falsehood of paradise.

"Master, master, she cried, have mercy on me!

Am I not worthy to be loved?"

But never once did her burden get shaken free.

Grievance was all she was and happiness seemed light years away.

The key to the world sat in a dusty corner of her life.

Fear of becoming whole set promises back

as if they were never spoken.

Once an angel, now an astray wanderer.

Her eyes spoke words of the heart she dare not reveal.

Finally, when time became endless and reality unknown

the bird opened her vast, neverending wings and began to fly.

Her soul reached out into the stars and

to be really free was a glorious spark in her now energetic being.

*Maisha Crawford*

# TAKE A LOOK

Look at yourself,
see the golden brown sister in the mirror.
You're every teachers prodigy
and every parents dream.
You, with your long lean legs
and your perfectly smoothed feet.
The signs of someone who has gone places
and is going somewhere.
Going down the positive road of life
and taking those around with you.

Look at yourself,
see the golden brown sister in the mirror.
Those eyes, those wonderful eyes.
Painted with the loveliest of dark brown.
Eyes that are always giving people
a sense of security.
And the eyes only accent more
the picturesque smile planted upon
your face.
A smile so bright that it lights up every
room you enter.
And this lovely smile is almost always
accompanied by your harmonious laugh.
A laugh seeming to make all troublesome
dilemmas disappear.

Look at yourself,
see the golden brown sister in the mirror.
You always know exactly what you want
and never afraid to work to get it.
When you speak,
everyone listens.

Not only is there stern importance
in whatever you may say,
there is also the remaining fact
that your voice intoxicates those around.
Making every man, woman and child
seem to hang on whatever words pass your lips.

Look at yourself,
see the golden brown sister in the mirror.
You are positively radiant:
an image of ancestors of the past,
great ones of the present,
and a hope for the future.
You know how to think for yourself
and will continue to do so.
Finding enjoyment in being yourself
and not portraying who or what
anyone else may want.

Look at yourself,
see the golden brown sister in the mirror.
You are peace, love and unity
rolled into one great being.
Keep on loving who you see in the mirror
and everyone else will too.

*Maisha Fishburne*

# CHANGING EXPERIENCE

When I was a young child, I had a crush on Donald Adams Andrews. I was the "ugliest" child in my school, and none of the boys even thought of going out with me. I was chubby with a Jheri-curl afro. I wore stupid clothes with these thick, dooky, brown-rimmed glasses. Well, Donald was fine. He was 5'4" (which was tall in my school) golden brown skin, and light brown eyes. I had a crush on him for a whole year. Donald had many girls that wanted to go out with him and he knew that he had them wrapped around his finger. I definitely knew he wouldn't choose me over the other pretty girls he had wrapped around his pinkie. Well, wouldn't you know, one day in computer class a couple of boys (including Donald) were talking. Donald said to me that if I lost some weight and lost my glasses, I would be pretty. I felt so bad after what he said to me that day. That statement made me feel like the ugliest girl in the world. After that statement, I felt that no one wanted me as their girlfriend. I also felt that I was ugly, so therefore I didn't care how I looked (clean or dirty). Plain and simple, I was ugly. Well, I grew out of that captive shell when I found God (Jesus). When I grew "up and out," the boys started to notice me. But, just because I was voluptuous didn't (in my eyes) make me pretty. It was the way I began to grow, it was how I held myself, it was when, how, what and where I did things, and it was the simple fact that I knew I was a beautiful, intelligent, African-American lady made by God's hands.

*Ayanna Saulsberry*

# UNTITLED


You,
So Damn Black and Proud
Wearin' red, black and green
And respect the Black Queen
But they can't even respect I, who took her perm out
All I get is "what's that about?"
If you loved yourself so damn much
Why in the hell, you need to get a touch
    Up—up—up and away
     In your processed land
    But what is natural
    The first woman and man
    The first impression
My life, Your life in recession
Or better yet just takin' a breath
That's all I'm tryin to do
For the little time that's left

*Adam Berry*

# UNTITLED

Lullaby of life on the wrong track
Two boys are the missing link
What is the most seductive thing in earth?
A question of constancy
A poisonous egg yolk
One course evidence of a simple test.
Eternal problem of an impression
Counterpoint the unexpected
sculpturing perfection
A small jump could go further than a long one
A professional secret.

*Jennifer Clary*

# FALLING FROM FRIENDSHIP

Hey little girl,
Didn't you forget something?
Can't run back to get it now
This time it's gone for good
You lost it forever this time
Pretty girl
Hey little girl
Where's your mommy now?
Why isn't she running to your rescue?
Don't you need her anymore?
She thinks you do
Can't you be her little girl
Just a little bit longer?
Hey little girl
You can't see me
But I know you hear me
Put down the bottle
And come sit on my lap.
Hey little girl
You don't have a daddy anymore
Let me protect you
I know you'll never forget me
I can love you
More than anyone has before
Hey little girl
Are you tired of being a little girl yet?
I can make you a woman
Isn't that what you want?
Hey little girl
Don't you want a friend like me?
I know you did
Or why did you enter the room?
Hey little girl.....
Why aren't you listening?

*Sophia White*

# WATCHING

Watching my life pass me by
As my sister constantly lies

Watching my mother
slowly die.
How awful, it makes me cry.

Watching my cousin
on a hot summer day
when I'm trying to get away.

Watching my world
so alone
watching my world
moan.

*Rebecca Rodriguez*

# GRADUATION POEM

A new chapter in our lives is begun:
memories of grammar school
will never be forgotten
even though we will be so far away
our footsteps in the halls will slowly
vanish
the echoes of our voices will no longer be heard
but our spirits will always linger about
reminding all of our existence
the roads we will travel
may not be the same
some will be paved with gold
and others with stone
we will walk the roads
open-minded and brave
ready and willing to step to
the light to receive future
endeavors with bright hearts

As we depart here today
bidding each other fond wishes
of farewell, but definitely not good-bye,
we end the first segment
of our lives and stand
tall at the threshold that
opens to a new life

*Aaron Williams*

# I GAZE

I gaze at the clear
wine waters of the ocean
as they brush over the white sands
of Cancun.

The mild waters moan
in ecstasy. An abnormal
emotion of the lost souls
at sea.

I gaze at my dimension,
a place where I lay. A bright light
breaks through the dark grey clouds.

An opportunity for me to
break free, but I cannot.

I am bound in strong
heavy metal chains, with my back
against a stone cold mossy wall.

I gaze at the Devil.
The source of all evil.
Only here to kill, steal, and destroy.
Not me, Devil, Not me.

I gaze at the undone accomplishments
of the unfortunate.
Winos, Drunks, Prostitutes, and
Abusers.
How can I get away?

I gaze into the heart
of the impassive person.
Their heart stone cold,
fragile and delicate.
Such a heart made-up,
make believe, fake, phony,
and unbelievable.

I gaze
My gaze

It flows into complete darkness,
the symbol of impurities
and wrong doing of men.

My gaze goes every which way.

Maybe a church where the pastor
believes in Holy Lust
or
where fathers rape
their own blood.

Everytime you turn on the tube
there's a report of a tragedy.

I'm tired of this.
Ain't nothing left
but,
a gaze.
So I gaze,
I gaze,
I gaze.

*Karl Osis*

# THE SEARCH

I sit and stare into an utter void
In search of the slightest of emotions.
I delve into a soul that seems long dead.
Once this place flowed with insane passions
That burned and chilled my mind relentlessly.
But now there is nothing—I am alone.
Yet, I continue to search endlessly.
Suddenly, a light through the darkness shone.
A light of immaculate symmetry.
Minuscule yet infinitely complex.
Strength fading, I reach for this artistry.
It infuses my mind as we conflux,
      And in its power I evolve, expand.
      It's clear now, I have power unrestrained.

# ASCENDANCE

**2**

*Adrienne Philia Samuels*

# THE ESSENCE OF FOREVER
*A Personal Manifesto*

I am a part of an eternal whole. My ancestors left me their memories, strengths, knowledge, and essence. They are powerful, therefore, I too am powerful.

I remember when my Egyptian people studied the stars and made the world's first calendar. I remember how I planned and built the pyramids of Giza. I created the Sphinx. I wrote the Bible. I am Jesus. I invented the long bow. I created language, mathematics, science, and history. I died when forced into slavery. I triumphed when my children overcame the imprisonment.

I am born with the memories, strengths, knowledge, and essence of my ancestors. My hands are mine, yet not. I can feel the razor-like cuts received from reaching into cotton. I remember the ropes, the whips, the chains, the hopes.
I am stronger because of this.

**But wait, there's more.**

I gave Edison the idea of electricity. I invented peace, mops, dust pans, bricks, fans, irrigation, collard greens, chitterlings. All are originally mine. Invention, beauty, and peace are inherent to my nature. It is impossible for me to create chaos.

I am my mother. Her mother, her mother and her mother. I am Melva, Madear, and Mary. Mother, Grandmother, and Mother of All. I have always been and will always be this way.

**Do you doubt this?**

Ask your question, hear my answer and be enlightened.

How long have I been and will I stay? I will tell you.

Count the stars in the sky. When that is done, count every grain of sand on the beach. When this is done, count the drops of water in the ocean. When you have completed that, count every snowflake that has fallen and is yet to fall. Now count them again. Perhaps now you understand. **I am forever.**

*Victoria Cammon*

# UNTITLED

Black Is powerful.
Black is powerful.
Not a doubt in mind to be.
Black is powerful.
Let me speak and explain to thee.
Black is powerful.
It stands like a statue.
Our style is unique
not of others you see.
Black is powerful.
It's the beauty of mankind.
Not decorated with words,
but naturalized by self.
Our race is a category
of much intelligence.
Black is Beautiful.
Black is Powerful.

*Maisha Crawford*

# SPEAKING IN TONGUES: A SKETCH

*Background info: English has become the official language of the United States and it is now illegal to use any words or phrases that don't fit the "American vocabulary." Joe sees a friend of his from college.*

Joe: Habari gani?

Sam: Shh! Quiet that down, don't you know we could get arrested.

Joe: I was just greeting you.

Sam: (whispering) Alright then. Ujima haberi gani.

Joe: (yelling) Why are you whispering? Are you afraid someone will find out that you celebrate Kwanzaa?

Sam: ( still whispering) No, I'm not afraid, I'm just not stupid. I don't want to go to jail.

Joe: Why would you go to jail?

Sam: Don'tcha know Kwanzaa is a felony. So is Hannukah, Cinco de Mayo and any other holiday with a name not found in Webster's Dictionary.

Joe: Man, this country is burnt up than a mug.

Sam: I know, but it's the law

Joe; And if the law isn't followed the olice-pay will come and take us away.

Sam: What'd you say?

Joe: Othing-Nay

Sam: Stop that! Stop it right now.

Joe: No, I'm not afraid. Damn the aw-lay.

Sam: (covering his ears) I'm not listening. I'm not listening. I might be named an accomplice.

Joe: An accomplice to what? My crime against the freaking constitution of los Estados Unidos?

Sam: Oui. I mean yes. See what you've got me doing?

Joe: Yeah, I got you breaking the freaking laws and I love it man!

*Michael Sit*

# NOTE ON ENGLISH AS THE OFFICIAL LANGUAGE

Look this country is suppose to be a "melting pot." But I don't see that happening. My mother and father were pretty successful back in Hong Kong, Taiwan. They had money and a pretty good life. But they came to this country because of schooling, because the schooling in Asian countries cost money. And schooling at Hong Kong, Taiwan cost a lot and they also wanted me to learn English, the language of "success." The way of the future. I had to go to bilingual classes because I couldn't understand a word of English. And I felt left out, awkward. Now that I've learned the language, it doesn't seem much now. And people who own restaurants and stores they also know English. They don't speak it fluently, but they know and understand it, which goes to show that language can do a lot for someone. But in doing so I lost a little part of that Asian boy who came to this country speaking Chinese with his long black hair. In order to gain something, I lost something. And like my parents, I will also be handicapped. I can't walk to Chinatown because I'll feel awkward. Just like my first few years in the U.S.

*Robert Cardenas*

# SOCIALIST CLIQUE

The sun is mine when it's in my mind. The way it shines, it burns my mind.
You feel true when you feel blue. I can't tell you of the tales I've been told.
I can't tell you of who I've tried to hold. Morality was
uprooted when society was diluted. I am not looking for the clearest
conscience. I am just looking for the best that functions. Justice is no more
in our time. Maybe it will make a cameo appearance in the year 3000,
but it is in very large doubt. There is a very slim chance of mercy for all
minorities. Yet, it comes with the package. I will never feel the satisfaction
of being accepted. Yet, I have so much bibliography of being rejected. To tell
a tale of a caress, or the rumor that follows the slap which goes hand in
hand with trust. When we grow up, make sure your sensitive mind is open.
To be civil is to be good. To follow anarchy is to alienate brotherhood. I am
trying to construct society as a gothic architect. Not to be your president next
to elect.
Or, to be the mirror we do not reflect. Can we bare pain and forgive.
Can we tell the story we try to live. You should never trust anyone but
yourself. You will find it is more than a big help. I am not asking you to
believe me. I am just asking the morals of society to leave me. Lifted like a
baby in the arms of a person I do not know. Wishing for infinity the moment
will last, yet it still goes. Living in a world we did not choose. Having the
wrong people in society rule. Open your mind wide, if you want to find what
you try to hide. Release me. Us. From this repressed, useless people that make
up this socialistic clique.

*Farideh Karadsheh*

# UNTITLED

Man molested youth and
said it was normal
Man stole money and
claimed it was his
Man rapes women for the
sake of future leaders
    and doused fires,
    became men,
    joined the army,
    the navy,
    the airforce
became all they could be
in their military

Man went 20,000 leagues under the
    sea,
not to mention the man on the
    moon,
The man who shot J.F.K.
Or, the man who wasn't there although
he said he would be . . .
    another man born,
    another dead.
Man will be honored and
    praised
and made out to be god
Man will always . . . always use his
"brains" to get to
    the top
Man is mayor, but sells crack
Man teaches youth about
    guns, drugs, guns, drugs . . .
    stashed away in his

briefcase
   (man is what you make him)
Man created offspring and
left nine months later
Man became father and
was called daddy
Man threw punches,
    fought for his woman
Man became suited to suit himself
Man invented
Man abandoned
Man demanded
Man is useless
a man is powerful
and typical
and smart
and pathetic, and a man.

*Candice A. Murphy*

# UNTITLED

Far off in the middle of the ocean was an island called Zetra. On this island was a beautiful village called Aracelia.

Aracelia was home to three women. Their names were Jalyn, Kaman, and Leeyen. Jalyn, Kaman, and Leeyan lived in luxury. They each had their own houses, all the clothes and enough food to last them for a very long time. Even though they had such riches, they were very mean to the peasants who lived in villages nearby. They did not allow anyone to enter the golden gates surrounding Aracelia.

One day, a peasant girl named Janine woke up and found her baby brother, Elias, sick. Janine and Elias had not eaten for a very long time. Scared, Janine dressed her brother and herself and headed for Aracelia. Janine knew how the three women of Aracelia treated peasants. But thought if she explained that the pair had not eaten for a long time, and that Elias was getting sick, she was sure that Kaman, Jalyn, and Leeyan would let her in and give her some food.

It was a long walk to Aracelia from Solka village, but when she saw the golden gates surrounding Aracelia, she ran the last steps to them holding Elias in her arms.

When she got there she was unpleasantly greeted by Kaman. Janine explained to Kaman about her baby brothers condition but Kaman laughed and said "No way are you getting in here." "He is so sick, look," Janine said as she pulled the blanket from over Elias, revealing his pale face. "I'm definitely not letting you and that thing in here," Kaman said, and walked away.

After days of pleading with Kaman, Jalyn, and then Leeyan, Janine gave up and started walking back home.

The next day while Leeyan, Jalyn, and Kaman were having a picnic together, talking about the many peasants they have turned away they noticed that they began to tremble. The whole village was shaking. They just ignored it, but then they felt another tremble, this one much stronger and louder than the first.

They grabbed each other in fear until it was all over. When they looked around they noticed nothing left standing. "Our house! Where will we live," said Jalyn. "What will we do for food," Leeyen cried. "Look, our clothes are all rags," Kaman yelled. The golden gate surrounding Aracelia crumbled to the ground.

The God Patrick came from the sky and told the women that they were being punished for their behavior towards peasants and they will now spend the rest of their lives as peasants.

*Jeff Daitsman*

## DEFIANCE

See the death
See millions die
We must rise up
We must defy
Man beat to death
In '92
You're just lucky
It wasn't you
Youth gunned down
In '94
We must not take this
Anymore

See the death
See millions die
We must rise up
We must defy
Rodney King
Bo Lucas too
Jason Collins
Next is you
Police Brutality
More and more
We must take action
Not just deplore

See the death
See millions die
We must rise up
We must defy

*Zeeshan Shah*

# ASCENDANCE

quit
scraping and scratching at the bare shreds of our time together
rant and rave ALL yu want
I'm going to leave today
          there is NO WAY
yu could stop me so
call the cops on me
if your needs be but
don't take this lightly
becuz its not slightly
                    that im annoyed
but with this constant degradation
you ve just destroyed
                    what could have been
something of MERIT ?
something of MERIT ?
                    a progression that was
                    unchosen
its been unwanted
and the digression
               desired
Fools who
can't read
Fools
who can't read
have known better taste
than so called critics
full of artistic
                    politics
madness
          but you make my mind trip
with your white chick
                    dis
position

Unconditioned
was I to this
insult
    which obviously was the
result
of all my toils
        with INK
        with INK
        my voice
TRYing desperately
for your acceptance ?
  your acceptance ?
I'm forging a new ground that's IT
tired of this decadence
I'm saying I'm
TIRED of this decadence
          so

ARE YU READY
ARE YU READY
        PAY ATTENTION
to ASCENDANCE
      ascend
to levels unexplored
       ascend
to free thoughts
NO more
    paranoia
about these people
      or
   those people
      or
   them
—free your mind and your ass will follow—
please
   please
      did yu need me to beg or
should I break your legs ?
Or

are there
>            compromises
compromises
we can reach
as to where
I can preach
>            I can preach while yu LISTEN
YU LISTEN
HA!

it does go both ways
>                        compromise that is
has NO do not enter
>                sign on it
or a one way ARROW
as you SHOULD know
>                        all I'm asking
is will yu let me grow?
or is it necessary
for the height
>            of my style
to be stunted?
>                becuz in the past
>                over quarrels we ve
only grunted
>            yes its begun
the ASCEND DANCE
>                        yes like a run
in the pantyhose
of your ESTABLISHED
>                        SO CALLED
>                            standards
well then
>        I shall
>            meander
away
>    meander
away

        and leave your
weak crumbling
plastic
        bumbling
logic (?)
        beLOW
and dance
ascend dance

*Yoni D. Zeigler*

# I REPRESENT

I REPRESENT,
A NATION OF AGGRAVATION,
NEVER BE REPRESENTED BY
LEE PRESS ON WEAVE BE LIKE A BARBIE BLEACH SKIN
   MENTALITEE.
I REPRESENT
A GENERATION RAISED ON OPEN PIT SAUCE SANDWICHES
WITH DREAMS OF BEING SOUL TRAIN DANCERS.
LOVE,
PEACE,
AND,
SOOOOOOOOUL!
SOLD,
FOR A POCKET FULL OF, rED,
wHITE,
and bLUE.
RAISE RIGHT HAND.
FACE FLAG,
WORSHIP A LAND BUILT ON THE BACKS OF THE ORIGINAL
MAN.
I REPRESENT
REVELATIONS SCRIBBLED ON SCROLLS ABOUT SOCIETYS'
RACIAL HYPOCRISY.
NEVER WILL I BE REPRESENTED
BY THE EYEWITNESS NEWS,
SHOWING ME AS SOME FOOL,
bANGING,
sLANGING,
cLOWNING,
fROWNING,
cOMPLAINING,
BUT NEVER cHANGING.
wONDERING wHY,

LIKE WE THE ONLY ONES THAT'S GETTIN' HIGH,
HAVEN'T SEEN A BLACK MAN CRY,
NEVER HAVING AN ALIBI.
CORRUPTING YOUNG MINDS,
BABY MAKA',
OUT OF CONTROL?
NO, THIS IS NOT THE CASE.
I REPRESENT
REPARATIONS,
SEGREGATION,
A SO-CALLED EMANCIPATION,
THAT GOT US LOSING FACE,
TO WIN THIS RAT RACE.
FRENCH KISSING DERRIERES,
WHILE YOU STILL GET COLD STARES.
BEING FORCED INTO PROJECTS
WHICH WAS A PROJECT
TO INJECT VIOLENCE AND
MAKE US
NEGLECT OUR INTELLECT.
GOT YOU SCREAMING "SARDINES IN A TIN CAN HAS MORE
SPACE THAN I HAVE."
SENDING,
preachers,
politicians,
and DRUGpushers,
TO REDEEM OUR SOULS.
SOLD FOR A POCKET OF, rED,
wHITE,
and bLUE,
100$ GYM sHOES.
ALL-STAR dreams,
quick crEAM,
european FANTASIES.
AFRICA FOR THE AFRICANS,
but NO PLACE FOR me.
 CAUSE I BE THAT NIGGA
FROM THE CENTA' OF NATURE.

SO TRY IF YOU MUST
TO HUMILIate,
SEPERate,
PENEtrate.
FOR YOUR OWN SAKE
you betta WAKE UP,
BEFORE THE MASSES OF BRONZE WARRIORS
CREEEEP UP ON YOUR CATHEDRAL OF UNJUST,
THEN YOU WILL HAVE TO PAWN YOUR POCKET OF RED
WHITE AND BLUE,
to save your own SOUL.
I REPRESENT A NATION OF AGGRAVATION!!!!!!!!!!

P.S.
TAKE HEED TO THE WORDS I WRITE, CAUSE YOU MIGHT
NEED THIS WHILE WE ARE IN THE MIDST OF REVOLUTION
BY: THE SUPREME DIVA

*Nia Lawrence*

# Umoja

*Fifteen-year-old Maya Richmond, an African American, and her father Justin, a professor who teaches Western Civilization at a university, prepare for the arrival of Dr. Zakiya Atukwe, a visiting professor from Ghana, and her teenage son Yehoshua. A discussion between father and daughter makes it clear that Justin is uncomfortable with the notion of his African roots; indeed, he feels that Dr. Atukwe is exotic and foreign. Maya contrasts his conservatism with her own fervent wish for cultural identity. When the Atukwes arrive, the professors plan a university event in the living room. Maya takes Yeshoshua to another room, where it becomes clear that they have met in the past and are secret boyfriend and girlfriend.*

DR. ATUKWE: (takes a deep breath) Ok, according to my notes, we start the course off with part one, "The Beginning." That's my detailed, two week explanation of the ancient Egyptian civilization. I'm finished with my syllabus. Here.

(She pulls out a stapled packet of paper and hands it to him.)

JUSTIN: (He looks over the packet and shakes his head.) Besides, this states that Egypt was the beginning of modern civilization. I thought that we had talked about this before. Everyone knows that the first civilizations started in Greece and Rome. You'll have to modify this part.

DR. ATUKWE: No, I've done extensive research on this. I'm positive that the first civilizations grew from ancient Egypt. I thought that you knew that the purpose of this class was to make sure that students realized that Egypt was a part of Africa and that that is where most of our roots are traced.

JUSTIN: There's no way in the world that all modern civilizations come from Africa. That's unheard of.

DR. ATUKWE: But it's the truth. ·
(JUSTIN shakes his head and sighs)

JUSTIN: Let's move on and come back to this later. What about the second part of the course?

DR. ATUKWA: (uneasily) The second part of the course is still unclear to me. It's half yours and half mine. I understand that I have the first part. You have yet to give a complete course description. You know it's due two weeks before school starts.

JUSTIN: (annoyed) I know. It'll be done on time. You don't have to be concerned about me. Just make sure your own work is taken care of.

DR. ATUKWE: You are wrong. I do have to be concerned about your work. We are working together you know. (Pause)

JUSTIN: You're right, you're right. Hey, how about we take a break. I'm a little thirsty, I need a drink. How 'bout you?

DR. ATUKWE: Yes. I would like a cup of lemonade, please. (hands him her empty cup.)

JUSTIN: One lemonade it is. The pitcher is in the dining room. I'll be right back.

(He turns to leave. Just as he reaches the door separating rooms, the lights come up in the dining room, revealing YEHOSHUA and MAYA kissing. The door opens and they separate, but not in time. JUSTIN has seen them. MAYA's mouth drops in shock and YEHOSHUA let's out a sigh and drops his head.)

JUSTIN: Oh my god! What is going on here? (Slams cup on the table)

MAYA: Daddy it's not as bad as it looks. See Ye—

YEHOSHUA: Aw man.

JUSTIN: Don't you tell me how it looks! I saw it! What were you doing?

(Meanwhile, DR. ATUKWE is in the living room listening to what is going on in the dining room and is becoming very concerned. She looks up from her papers, rises, and goes into the dining room.)

YEHOSHUA: (to MAYA) Let me explain. (to JUSTIN) Mr. Richmond, Maya and I—

(DR. ATUKWE enters room.)

DR. ATUKWE: What is going on in here? (to JUSTIN) Why are you yelling?

JUSTIN: Your son was trying to molest my daughter!

DR ATUKWE: (raising her voice) That's outrageous, how dare you accuse my son of something like that. I want to know what is going on, now.

JUSTIN: (he looks at her as if he doesn't believe what she's saying) Don't speak to me like that.

DR. ATUKWE: How can you tell me how to speak to you, I am not your child.

JUSTIN: But you're in my house and I demand respect in it.

(DR. ATUKWE begins to make a come back but is interrupted by the entrance of MELISSA through the back door of the dining room.)

MELISSA: (groggily, she has been woken from her nap. Yawns.) What's going on? All this yelling woke me up from my nap.

MAYA: (resorting to her mother for help.) Mom, Dad walked in—

JUSTIN: (interrupting) I came into the dining room for some cups and (to DR. ATUKWE) and your son and (To MELISSA) and our daughter were kissing in this room!

(Looks of shock, eyebrows raised and confusion lasts for approximately three seconds.)

DR. ATUKWE: What's the meaning of this?

YEHOSHUA: Mom, I can explain—

DR. ATUKWE: You have a lot of explaining to do.

MELISSA: Well, I sure do want to hear Maya's side of this story. (turns to MAYA) Can you give me some sort of explanation? You weren't really kissing were you?

MAYA: Mom, Mom, I've been—

JUSTIN: (hounding her) Been what?

MAYA: (uneasily she doesn't know how to explain that she's been seeing YEHOSHUA) Well you see, I—

(Pause as she tries to find the right words)

YEHOSHUA: What Maya is trying to say is that she and I have been seeing each other for four months.

DR. ATUKWE: You knew each other all along?

JUSTIN: Even when you were out there? (points to living room) How did you—

YEHOSHUA: (to DR. ATUKWE) When you told me last week that you were coming here, I knew that I would see Maya. We had planned to tell you all this evening, but—

JUSTIN: (cruelly) But what?

MAYA: (snaps back) But you made it clear that you wouldn't want me to see him. Even though I didn't even tell you a thing about him.

JUSTIN: That's absolutely right. I forbid you to see that boy anymore!

DR. ATUKWE: That boy is my son.

MAYA: Yehoshua is my boyfriend, Dad, whether you like it or not.

(When JUSTIN hears her say the word "boyfriend," he cringes. YEHOSHUA smiles at her.)

JUSTIN: I just don't think that this is going to work.

MAYA: Why don't you just say what you mean.

DR. AYUKWE: (to MAYA, confused) What are you talking about?

JUSTIN: I don't think that Maya is ready for this — for a relationship yet.

MAYA: That's not what you mean.

(There is a pause and MELISSA and MAYA look to JUSTIN for an answer.)

JUSTIN: Well, what I mean is that she's not old enough to date. She's only fifteen.

MELISSA: Justin, she'll be sixteen in two months.

JUSTIN: That's not the point, she's not sixteen yet. I set the age at sixteen. If she can't abide by my rules, then I'll set the age back farther.

MAYA: That's not the reason you don't want me to see Yehoshua.

YEHOSHUA: Maya, I don't think that you should bring that up now.

JUSTIN: I just want the best for my daughter.

DR. ATUKWE: Are you implying that my son is not the best for your daughter?

JUSTIN: What I'm implying is that I don't want any child of mine going to live with some African boy. I want the best for my daughter.

DR. ATUKWE: And you don't think that I want the best for my son? Believe me, I am not thrilled to hear that he is seeing some American girl, all that I've heard about them.

MELISSA: (raises eyebrows) What've you heard about American girls?

DR. ATUKWE: Only that they're all lazy, do—nothing prostitutes, but I see that's not true in all cases.

JUSTIN: (frustrated) I just don't like the whole idea of this. (raises his voice) I don't want my child being dragged off to Africa to be forced to be married before she's ready and have tons of kids and stay bare foot and pregnant.

MAYA: Dad, how do you know I'm going to marry Yehoshua?

JUSTIN: You'll probably be forced in to marriage.

DR. ATUKWE: (shocked) Oh. So these are the stereotypes that go around about us in America. In all my nine years here, I've never heard one of them.

MELISSA: (to DR. ATUKWE) We've had this talk all ready, I'm just sorry that you had to hear all of this.

DR. ATUKWE: I guess it was good to get all this out in the open. Now I know how you feel, and you know that all those rumors are false.

(JUSTIN shrugs as if he doesn't really care. YEHOSHUA turns to MAYA with his back to the group so that no one else hears.)

YEHOSHUA: I'm glad that was all straightened out. I told you that your dad was rational.

JUSTIN: No, I can't go on pretending like I don't care if this relationship goes on or not.

MELISSA: Justin, I think that we should just leave this alone. It's really Maya and Yehoshua's decision.

MAYA: (raising her voice) Thank you. Dad, I wish you would just leave us alone. Why is that so hard for you?

JUSTIN: Don't you dare raise your voice at me in front of our company.

MAYA: You really don't care. Why don't you tell them all the things you said before they came!

JUSTIN: (viciously) Shut up!

DR. ATUKWE: (annoyed and upset) It's getting late. I think Yehoshua and I should be on our way. (turns to MELISSA) It was very nice to meet you. Thanks for everything.

MELISSA: I'll see you out.

(MELISSA leads YEHOSHUA and DR. ATUKWE through the dining room door and into the living room. She pantomimes showing them out and expressing an apology.)

(Meanwhile . . .)
JUSTIN: I don't believe you did this to me.

MAYA: (with an attitude) Did what?

JUSTIN: You embarrassed me in front of my co-worker. How could you say those things?

MAYA: How could I say those things? I don't believe you said all those stupid things to Dr. Atukwe.

JUSTIN: I'm not having this, you have to show me some respect.

MAYA: You don't deserve respect.

JUSTIN: (roars) I told you I wouldn't have this in my own house, now get out of my sight!

(MAYA jumps when her father yells)

JUSTIN: Get out, get out NOW!

(MELISSA comes back in)

MELISSA: Stop the yelling, stop it all now!

(Everyone looks to MELISSA)
MELISSA: (to JUSTIN) You're acting like a child. I don't want to hear anymore about this, do you understand? Maya, go to your room, I have to talk to your father, alone.

(MAYA rises and walks to the door of the dining room. She turns back as if she was about to say something.)
MAYA: (softly) I thought you'd understand, Dad.

(MAYA then turns and leaves the room and the lights go out on stage.)

# DREAMING IN BLUE LIGHTS

3

*Audrey Conley*

# LOVE . . .

Is sharing and caring.

Is commitment.
(Being there for him or her
through the toughest struggles.)

Love is . . .

Being your partner's best friend
(It isn't just knowing who that person is!)

Love is understanding

Love is pain and misery
Happiness and sadness
Sorrow and Loneliness

Joy

*Kambi Iverson*

# !!!!!!!RED!!!!!!!

Talking to you on the phone last night,
   I wondered if you thought of me as a puppet.
      Were you pulling my strings????????????????????????

Leading me on a path straight to destruction.
      "Don't fall in love,
   It could get a lot of people hurt," you said.

But I had already started down that road.
   Talking to you, I realized that you wouldn't be there
   when this path ends.

If I could open my heart
   I would share how you fill my dreams every night.

     The hugs, the kisses,
      the arguments and the smiles.
       You came into my life with a flash,
      And already my feelings for you are so strong.

       Now I think I love you.
      But the question is,
     will you ever LOVE me????????????

*Brendan Mattson*

## LICKS OF LIPS

They say it's not too wise
    To dedicate your smiles to eyes
or scatter laughs on confidence
    like dancers' bodies speaking blue streaks.
Licks of lips set fires in minds,
    flickered eyelids whisper interest
words are abstract, hollow mumbles,
    fleeting intangible moans and consonance.
You are an animal, fixed and final
    whose flickered eyelids whisper interest
like sweating bodies screaming blue streaks.
    Time is abstract, nonexistent,
measured by the undying repetition of motion!
    You are an animal, fixed and continuous.
Time is music, sex and heartbeats.
    Words are fleeting hollow moans.
No words are numbers, can't mean time,
    it's licks of lips set fires in minds.

*Cristalle Bower*

# FIRST KISS

It was about 90 degrees that day. I remember a sort of violet-blue sky, the kind of sky in which you know for sure the little ones would catch lots of lightning bugs. I sat with Jody, my boyfriend of two days. We were still in that giggling-like-a-schoolgirl-stage . . .or at least I was. We were sitting on those little benches in the park, a few feet from the fountain. The night was perfect. A night that anything could and probably would happen. We were sitting there, speaking of everything and nothing at all. I couldn't help myself from constantly watching his full, pinkish lips. I knew that I would feel them soon. I had to be patient. I especially loved it when Jody said the word, "look." If you paid close enough attention, as I was, you could see his tongue flicker in and suddenly out of his mouth. He had the most beautiful mouth. The kind of mouth you could penetrate for an eternity and beg for more. Well, we sat there for a good half hour, until it was kind of getting late and time to head back. I was only nine years old. The whole walk home was maddening. Each of us anticipating the kiss. Thinking of it in our minds. Each of us surprisingly silent. As we neared the steps leading to the door, we sat on my porch. We said our "goodbyes" and "I had a nice time" crap, then we kissed. The approach wasn't all that great, neither was the delivery, but it was satisfactory because the lips that I had daydreamed about for days were finally touching mine. When you finally get something you've been desiring, it's kind of hard to pretty much think of anything else.

*Marlena R. Irizarry*

# A Spring Day

Today, gravity seems to have no effect

Rain slowly drops from the heavenly skies above
As the sun begins to set in the east.

Early morning dew smells
As sweet as a kiss of honey.

With the cool, misty air,
One can feel the means of life from deep within.

As you look around,
You can see trees careening against the wind.
And you can hear the lustrous sounds of nature.

A spring day can be so simple
Yet, so beautiful

Life would be better and brighter
If it were as wonderful as a spring day.

*Jason Montemayor*

# QUESTIONS........

Warm summer nights, and
cool wind-worn evenings.
    Interlocking hands holding
each other as if they were life.
Under the shade where lovers lay and
 young children play,
    dreaming in blue lights
through star-filled nights and
days, filled with joy.

    Clouds and pillows, one
on top of the other, begging
the question;

Which is lighter, feathers
or clouds?

  In tiny puddles
of teardrops, filled with sadness and
forgetful memories,
I stare at my reflection.

*Melissa Molitoris*

# LOST LOVE

I lost you, my dear love, to another girl
You went away without even looking back
What she has that I don't, I really can't be sure
Won't you tell me what it is that I lack?

There is one thing, now that I think of it
It is your sweet love that she's acquired
She was happily hit by the bullet
That your gun of love has fired

But one thing I have that she so sadly lacks
Is the ability to endure the pain
Cause when you hurt her and her heart cracks
Only her loneliness is left to reign

I will say this once, and one time only:
Just because I'm alone, doesn't mean I'm lonely

*Edith E. Bucio*

# THE AWAKENING OF THE FOREST

Stunned you stare at me.
Your eyes widen at the
sight at my breasts.
The paleness of my naked skin
makes you wonder. . . .

Wonder
what it would be to feel me,
wonder if I should shiver
at your touch.
Wonder if my thighs are
smooth and soft.

Do not wonder.
Let your hands and body
go wild,
just as your mind has.
Come to me.
Satisfy that desire.

*Felix Flauta*

# LET'S DEFINE LOVE

Goo goo names and voodoo dolls
Window shopping at the mall
"Let's share one drink with two bendy straws!"
All ideas grown from his one flaw.

Ridiculous as this past seems
Now, but it wasn't so bad back then
To live his life in a backward bend
And excite the breathing of a friend.

He remembers this past in a daydream:

"Goodbye my dear, take care, take care,
Don't let that brainwashed, beautiful head get lost."

"I'll do as I please and attract the moths
but if I'm lost I'll find my way back here."

And so he followed her gentle wish
And they departed with a kiss.

\*   \*   \*   \*   \*

Somewhere, somehow, someplace, someway
He gets shot in the head on this perfect day
His brain gets lost outside in the rain
Washed away his emotions and the pain.

Her eyes are different after he's found some pieces
She's different now that he's not whole
(And in his head a big gaping hole!)
She leaves him then with a kiss
Granting not his final wish.

In that vast ocean, they say there's how many fish?

Does he dare say, "Well that's over, I never cared?"
(And from that hole, blood running from his hair!)

He believes in constant motion, moving everywhere
But holding on to stability lost, he grips and tears
Out hair.

\*   \*   \*   \*   \*

"How beautiful you are, my friend
How long it seems to last until we end,"
Sharp memories of this voice he calls
And holding the image of himself
He breaks the head off the voodoo doll.

*Sylvia Pyrich*

# WANDERER

Laying close to an invasion,
Striking the mutiny inside my heart.
I feel an understanding for the methodist,
preaching daily without comfort.
I caress his thorns of lust.
Beaming with homesickness.
Daring to release the cheap heaven he signed himself into.
The door stirs with disbelief
over his ferocious misuse of the book.
His tears drop into the pages.
Bowing his head with surrender,
he slams the book shut and smiles with relief.
Caressing my reflection in the mirror,
he gazes hard into my eyes.
Intimidating my presence.
With a possessed rage, his tormented soul
hurls the holy masterpiece against his reflection
in the shattered portrayal of broken vows.
His hair masks the madness in his face.
Yet, the eyes pierce through my reluctance
pounding his urge through my self control.
His long, pale hands invade my comfortable loneliness
grasping my arm with a dominating power.
While the sharp claws dig into my surrendering skin.
He breathes heavily, moaning with pleasure
as the nails scratch the first layer away.
He grabs my limp arm and drives my nails across his chest.
He ceases to breathe.
His previous outrage of hysteria,
is relieved by this ripping ecstasy we relish.
His skinny arms hold me tightly.
His eyes close to the illuminating atmosphere.
A destination of his dependability holds firm my grasping statue.
His captivating strength trembles
from the ethereal pleasure potion we sacrificed to each other.

*Dan Lavorini*

# LOVE AFFAIR

I feel the streets beneath my tired feet
The concrete being torn up behind me
The feel of the city soothes my body
The darkness spreading over
Finding places where the street lights are
forbidden to break the silence of night
Darkness that covers, caresses, kills
Careless night hiding the life of the Earth
Loving everything it holds
Conquering the day
I love it, too
So, still I walk
Walk alone in the darkness
Having a love affair with night

*Veronica Sansing*

# HONEY

*Simone Pater and her mother Celia and baby brother live in an apartment. Celia, a single parent, whose insecurity makes her feel that life is only valid with the company of a man, is constantly out on dates. Simone has little free life of her own, as she cares for her brother and is forced to accept the "adult" role in the family. As the play opens, Simone is preparing for her first date, with Sydney, a grocery delivery clerk. She explains her elation to her friend Retta on the telephone. Joy turns to bitterness when Celia appears and seems to have forgotten that she promised he daughter a night off from family responsibility.*

RETTA: (stares at SIMONE closely) Uh, my gosh, baby doll's turned into Cover Girlie. I never thought I'd live to see the day you'd wear mascara,

SIMONE: (Sarcastically) Funny.

CELIA: I helped her put it on.

RETTA: (looks at SIMONE'S lips) "Persian Ruby." I have that shade myself.

CELIA: Don't it look nice on her?

RETTA: Uh huh. And her hair. It looks so nice.

SIMONE: Can't take the credit for that either.

CELIA: I did it. Nice isn't it?

RETTA: Man, this must be some date. Looks like both you girls got lucky. Celia, who've you got to baby . . .

CELIA: (nervously) Simone, could you fix Retta and me some Diet Pepsi? There's a full bottle in the fridge.

SIMONE:(reluctantly) Yes, Celia. (heads towards the kitchen)

CELIA: Go ahead.

RETTA: That's okay. I'm not . . .

CELIA: And make sure you add lots of ice, It's really hot today. (SIMONE goes into the kitchen )

RETTA: What's with you? I'm not stayin' long. (No reply. CELIA puts her head down nervously and starts to fidget) Hold on. . . . You haven't told her have you?

CELIA: Sigh.

RETTA: (angrily) Celia, how could you? That's so mean. What are you gonna tell that poor girl when she finds out?

CELIA: I don't know. Everything was just happening so fast and . . .

RETTA: You're gonna break her heart.

CELIA: I know . . .

RETTA: Don't let me be the one to tell her. No. You know what? I'm gonna stay out of this.

CELIA: (curtly) Thank you.

RETTA: This is strictly between you and Simone and I don't wanna be here when she finds out.

(SIMONE enters holding two glasses of ice cold Diet Pepsi)

SIMONE: Here you go. (hands Celia her drink)

CELIA: Thanks.

SIMONE: And you. (walks over to Retta and there's a squeak from a squeaky toy that SIMONE steps on. She loses her balance and spills some of the cola on her shirt.)Oh, shit.

CELIA: Did you get any on you?

SIMONE: (disgusted) Yeah, all over my top. I stepped on Claudius's squeaky toy.

CELIA: Do you have anything else you can wear?

RETTA: Let me get that for you honey. (takes the glass from SIMONE)

SIMONE: I can wear my white top with the wooden buttons that I got last week.

RETTA: Some club soda will take those stains right out.

(The phone rings and CELIA makes a dash towards it.)

CELIA: I'll get. (picks up the phone) Hello?. . . (nervously happy) Oh hi. Um, could you hold on for a second? (to SIMONE) Go upstairs and change out of your top, honey. (SIMONE heads upstairs) Hello, Clive, (SIMONE stops ascending and hides behind the rails. There is a canned male voice coming from the telephone. It is CLIVE.)

CLI: Hey, Celia. Is there something wrong?

CELIA: It's nothing, really. My daughter, Simone, spilled some cola on her shirt. Did you get my page?

CELIA: Yes, I did. You paged me about ten minutes ago. Sorry it took so long for me to get back to you. I had to stop for gas.

CELIA: You mean you're on a car phone?

CLI: That's right.

CELIA: Oh, that explains all the static and the car horns.

CLI: I find that this phone comes in very handy for business calls. So, are you ready?

CELIA: Yep. Dressed and ready to go.

RETTA: (whispers angrily) Celia!

CLI: Great, do you like Italian food?

CELIA: Do I like Italian food? I love it.

CLI: I know this great restaurant in downtown Chicago.

CELIA: All the way in Chicago?

CLI: Sure. I'll be at your place soon. In about IO minutes. Is that okay for you?

CELIA: I'll be ready. Just come and blow your horn. I'll come out.

CLI: I guess I'll see you later then. Bye.

(SIMONE tip toes up the stairs.)

CELIA: Bye. (hangs up the phone)

RETTA: Honestly, Celia. I can't believe you did that to your little girl.

CELIA: Will you just shut up? What makes you think this is easy for me? I have feelings, too.

RETTA: Sure could have fooled me.

CELIA: I thought you were gonna stay out of this.

RETTA: Fine, fine. You want me to stay out of this? I'll stay out of it then. I won't even stay to hear you tell your own daughter that she can't go on her first date 'cause mama here wants to go on another date with another man she just met.

CELIA: It's not that simple. (CELIA hears SIMONE descending the stairs.)

Now you just shut up and let me handle this.
(SIMONE comes down the stairs in a white tops, She has a fake smile across her face.)

SIMONE: How does this outfit look? Does it look as good as the other tops did? (goes over to couch)

RETTA: You look wonderful. (looks at CELIA slyly) Doesn't she, Celia?

CELIA: (fake happiness) Yes, honey. You look beautiful. The white top looks much better than the ivory one did.

SIMONE: Good. I want to look absolutely perfect for my first date tonight. I don't want anything to spoil my plans. (RETTA and CELIA say nothing) Oh, Celia. Can I borrow your silver bracelet with the blue beads dangling from it? I think it'd go really well with what I'm wearing.

CELIA: Um, Simone, sit down. (CELIA goes over to the couch and sits down. SIMONE joins her.)

SIMONE: Yes?

RETTA: (getting up from her chair ) I think I'd better leave now. I've got so much work to do. (heads towards the door ) See you guys later. (stares at CELIA) Good luck. (Exits)

CELIA: Simone, I just received a phone call.

SIMONE: Yes?.

CELIA: It was Clive. He just told me that he's leaving for South Dakota tomorrow morning. And well . . .

SIMONE: And well what?

CELIA: Well, (stands up and paces the room ) since he's leaving tomorrow morning, he wants to take me out tonight.

SIMONE: And you said no, didn't you? Because you knew that I had plans to go out tonight. Something I've been waiting for for weeks.

CELIA: Simone, you have to realize that this, too, is something I've been waiting for for a very long time.

SIMONE: What? Another date?

CELIA: (turns from her and attempts to be cheerful) He wants to take me out to dinner.

SIMONE: And you said no, didn't you?

CELIA: He knows this nice Italian restaurant in downtown Chicago.

SIMONE: (more upset) And you said no, didn't you?

CELIA: (pleading) Will you please understand. This could be the right guy for me.

SIMONE: (On the verge of tears ) Please, Mom. Please tell me you said no. Please tell me that you told him that your daughter is going out on her first date. Something she's been waiting for all her life.

(CELIA does not answer but simply turns away. She takes a deep breath and folds her arms.)

CELIA: (coldly but with a lump in her throat) When Sidney arrives . . .

SIMONE: (very softly, shaking her head down in disbelief ) No, Mama . . .

CELIA: . . . I want you to tell him that you're sorry . . .

SIMONE: Please don't do this.

CELIA: . . . but you can't go out tonight. (pause) Your mother has a date.

SIMONE: (long pause, softly.) Damn you.

CELIA: (confused) What?!

SIMONE: (standing up. louder) Damn you! I said damn you!

CELIA: You watch your mouth young lady . . .

SIMONE: I'll say whatever I damn well please. I can't believe you sat here, looked me in the eyes and told me a bold face lie, expecting me to sit here and swallow it.

CELIA: What are you talkin' about?

SIMONE: You know very well what I'm talking about. I'm talking about that conversation that you and Mr. Wonderful just had. I heard every word you said to him.

CELIA: You were eavesdropping on me?

SIMONE: (mimicking her mother) Let's just say it was an A & B conversation and you didn't C me. I can't believe you would try to do something like this to me. You knew I wanted to go on this date so bad. I've been waiting for the longest and you're trying to screw it up.

CELIA: Will you listen . . .

SIMONE: You blew for a jerk who picks you up in a beauty salon.

CELIA: Simone, don't you understand? This could be the guy for me. He's nice, handsome, and he makes good money. He really could be the one.

SIMONE: But that's what you say about every guy who comes your way. That's probably what you said about Dad . . . and look where you two guys ended up.

CELIA: You leave your father out of this and I mean it . . . you have no idea what you're talkin' about.

SIMONE: (ignoring her mother ) He was probably "the one" a couple of years ago, but look at you two now. Divorced and miserable. You guys argued constantly . . .

CELIA: (terribly annoyed and frustrated ) Will you Shut up?! (pause) Do you know why I divorced your father? (SIMONE turns from CELIA) Your father and I had to get married because I was pregnant with you. From then on, he wanted no more children. Just a housewife that would cook and clean and keep him happy. Man, when your father said no more children, he meant no more children (pause) Simone, do you realize the countless number of abortions I've been through just so I could keep your father? Do you realize how many nameless children I had to kill just to keep our (makes quotation mark hand gestures ) "happy" home? You have no idea do you? When I was pregnant with Claudius, I refused to get an abortion. I swear your father got so mad. Mind you, he hated children, but he loved you very much. Then I wanted to get a job so I could support the family, That was too much for him.  He just couldn't stand the thought of another child and a working wife. So two months after your brother was born, Leroy bailed out on me. He simply couldn't take it anymore. I finally got little Claudius and my freedom. And, dammit, I'm making the most of it.

SIMONE: But at the expense of others? Celia, I'm sorry that you had to go through all that but it does not justify what you're trying to do. (defiantly) I'm going out with Sidney.

CELIA: You keep forgetting that I'm the mother and you're the daughter.

SIMONE: Well act like it! (pause)

CELIA: Fine. You want me to act like a mother? Then I'll act like a mother . . . (in a loud voice) Simone Marie Pater! You will remain home and take care of Claudius while I go out with Clive and there will be no—do you hear me—no back talk whatsoever. Now you know I can't afford a babysitter so you're all I've got right, now. (a car horn blows, CELIA goes over to the door and opens it to see who it is.) My date's here. (she readies herself for the date.) Now take good care of Claudius. I'll be home later on tonight. (Turns to open the door and looks back at Simone) Simone, he really could be the one for me. (no reply from SIMONE. CELIA turns away and leaves sadly. She stays on the front porch for a while and tries to look cheerful for CLIVE. She waves at a car from afar.) Coming Clive!

CELIA rushes off the porch. Simone closes the door and begins to cry softly. She sits down on the couch. She then pulls some tissue from a tissue box in the beauty case and begins to wipe her tears.

SIMONE: (sadly) Take care of Claudius! Take care of Claudius while I go out with the girls. Watch Claudius while I got out on another date with some dumb jerk I just met. Change his diaper—Wash his clothes. Give him a damn bath. That's all you ever say to me.

(SIMONE turns the beauty case towards her and looks in the mirror. Her mascara is running, She begins to wipe it off slowly and then begins to wipe all the make-up off her face with great force and anger. She throws the tissue on the ground and closes the beauty case with a slam. She picks herself up and goes over to the typewriting table. She picks up the box of typewriter ribbon, opens it and places the ribbon in the typewriter. She sits down at the table and places a sheet of paper in the machine. She begins to type during the soliloquy. What she is saying is what she is typing—)

SIMONE: In conclusion, no one really knows the true ranks of hierarchy in the kingdom of the bees between the queen bee and the worker bees. Some say that the worker bees hold the power. It is they who keep the queen bee supposedly captive so she can lay eggs. They are the ones who tend to the larvae and in result, create more bees to help them with the work and to protect the hive. The queen has a minimal amount of freedom compared to the workers once she begins to lay eggs. On the other hand, there are some who say that the queen bee holds the most power. Some even go as far to say that she's the absolute monarch. She is the one who gives work orders to the other bees so that they may keep her comfortable, maintain the hive and raise the larvae. She is the one who chooses whether there will be another queen bee to take her place or if there will only be a new colony of workers. All in all, no one is sure who deserves the title of "chief" in the bees world.

(SIMONE pulls the paper from the typewriter and places it at the bottom of a pile which she then staples together. In the background there is college music playing softly, then builds. A car horn blows and SIMONE throws her paper down. She hesitates and starts to walk towards the door. Claudius starts to cry from upstairs. SIMONE looks up towards the stairs and then looks at the front door.

SIDNEY: (offstage) Come on, Simone! We're waiting for you! Get a move on it!

SIMONE hangs her head down and walks towards the door. The lights fade as the baby continues to cry.

# EXCUSES! EXCUSES!

4

*Kathy Bardales*

# AT CHURCH

Sitting on a pew
thinking of
popcorn and
hats and
guys and
God - yeah - God.
Stand up
sit down
open to page . . .
And sing!
Everybody now!
Now kneel
praying and
thinking of
diets and
Oprah and
guys and
God - yeah - God.
Turn around
shake hands
smile
(Who are they?!)
Kiss your mom
Everybody now!
Get in line
behind the wig
the blue wig
hoping not to go to hell
Nice priest
Eat the bread
Sip the wine
Pray a lot.
Thinking about

dogs and
hats and guys and
God - yeah - God.
Peace be with you
oh okay.
Phew let's go.
Sign of the cross
Holy water
See ya.

*Stephanie Wheeler*

# CD JUNKY

CD's are usually $14.99
Who am I kidding? Am I out of my mind?!
The price is so high for all my favorite songs.
But when I go to buy them the lines are so long.
Maybe its God, just giving me a sign.
"You don't need CD's so don't stand in line."
"Go outside do anything but this."
"There's a world out there that you don't want to miss."

*Katie Solka*

# A CHRISTMAS STORY

"Oh, woe is me! What ever shall I do?" A plump elderly man sat by a crackling yule log, sobbing gently. Staring into his reflection in a red glass ornament, Santa Claus softly munched away on a candy cane. A quaint little old lady began comforting her husband, "Don't worry dear, Rudolph will turn up in time."

You see, Rudolph, Santa's only reindeer that can guide him through the foggy night sky, had abruptly disappeared without a trace two days ago. It was now five days until Christmas. Without Rudolph, Santa cannot fly his sleigh on Christmas Eve. Because of his disappearance, Santa Claus had sent out his elves, including me, to travel into millions of shopping malls with the terrible news. Christmas would be canceled unless Rudolph was found in time. Donner, one of Santa's reindeer, knew Rudolph loved Christmas very much and would not run off or get lost. It caught Donner's attention that the only one who would love to see the world rid of Christmas was the notorious grinch, The Abominable Snowman. Donner had a plan to go rescue Rudolph from the clutches of the beast. Santa and Mrs. Claus would never allow him to venture out looking for Rudolph. In fact, if Donner had mentioned the idea to anyone, they would have snitched on him. Why shouldn't we? The Abominable Snowman had been terrorizing the North Pole for as long as I could remember. It was WAY too dangerous! The brave little reindeer realized the possibility of never being heard from again, but made up his mind to rescue his buddy and save Christmas. No matter what. He began packing scarves, a map, and some food in a backpack. He thought he would bring one of Mrs. Claus' home baked pies. Late that night, Donner quietly left for the ice cliffs.

By 1:00 the next day, Donner reached the long range of ice cliffs. He took a look around the strange new land, with nothing but bone chilling ice formations surrounding him. As Donner continued, he could hear a faint chirping sound. He followed the sound to discover a little chickadee who had fallen into the snow. Donner thought this was no place for a helpless little bird, and without doing something the bird would die. He brushed off the snow covering the chickadee and picked it up. Donner dashed to a tree to shield himself from the icy wind. Setting up a tent, he decided it would be best to rest for a while. Wrapping the little bird up warmly, he placed some food in a small dish beside it. Donner woke up late in the afternoon, to the chirping of the chickadee. The little bird said, "My name is Chip and I was flying home for the holidays when this terrible storm hit. I was blown into these ice cliffs and buried under the snow just this morning. Thank you so much for coming to my rescue. Is there anything I can do in return to show my appreciation?" Donner explained the situation he was in and before he could finish, Chip, fluttering with excitement, interrupted him. "I can show you where the Abominable Snowman lives! He dwells in the ice caverns west of the Arctic Ocean. I do not know what his weakness is, but I have heard he has a sweet tooth. I will accompany you in your quest to save Rudolph." Donner was quite relieved at this news. They decided on waiting until morning to resume their search.

Bright and early the next morning, with three days left until Christmas, Donner and Chip set out for the ice caverns. They arrived at the mouth of the cavernous lair at midday, with the icy ocean waves crashing in the distance. Chip, being familiar with the cavern's maze, led Donner through the crystal formations. Donner tripped over huge footprints imbedded in the ice. They came to a mesa where the footprints went in all directions. "It appears we are in the heart of the cavern," Chip whispered softly. Just as Donner was about to respond, the staggered ice hanging from the ceiling began shaking. The Abominable Snowman was approaching, with the hideous roar of the beast echoing against the cavern walls. As the shadow of the Abominable Snowman peeked around the corner, Donner stepped back and swallowed hard. Chip was perched on his antlers. The monstrous ogre stepped into the mesa's edge. Some of Donner's belongings fell out of his backpack, making a loud noise. The beast noticed Donner and Chip and began to thunder toward them. Donner looked at his supplies, a few pans, a map and a pie. He remembered Chip's tip, "The beast has a sweet tooth." Just as the Abominable Snowman was about to reach down and smite them, Donner picked up Mrs. Claus' pie and whipped it right in the monster's eyes. The beast flew backwards, blinded by the lemon merangue filling. It was stumbling at the edge of the mesa when Donner rushed over and butted the beast in it's stomach. The beast let out a roar as it fell into the crevasse which was followed by a chilling splash from the icy river below.

Donner and Chip quickly ran to the tunnel. They found Rudolph trapped in a cage of icicles. Donner picked up a pan from his sack and smashed the icicles into a thousand pieces. Rudolph was overcome with joy as he leapt out of the ice. As Chip guided them back to the stormy outside weather, they realized it was already nighttime. Now there were two days left until Christmas and in order to make it they had to hurry. Rudolph guided Donner and Chip as they flew through the snowy sky. They arrived at Santa's house the next morning, and Santa ran out into the snow in his pajamas to hug the three heroes. Santa, overwhelmed with happiness, immediately sent us elves to malls across the world with the joyous news that Christmas would not be canceled. Santa held a huge Christmas Eve party to which Chip and his family were invited. Night fell, we began packing the sleigh with presents. As the reindeer flew across the moon, the sight of a red light guiding them assured everyone that Christmas was back to normal.

*Nina Washington*

# DEAR TEACHER

Mrs. Price, I was absent two days ago because I woke up and saw something running around my room. So, I didn't get up. Then, I saw it go out of the room. So I got up. I went into the bathroom and saw a horse in my tub. She asked me to give her the soap. I looked at her, Mrs. Price, and put her out. Then I went down stairs and saw my cat dancing! Then I knew I was going crazy! So, I went to get something to eat, and do you know what I saw! That horse was eating all of my cereal!! So that is why I am absent and why I am calling you from the mental hospital.

*Melody Martin*

# EXCUSES! EXCUSES!

Ohmigosh! My homework is due!
The teacher will tear me in two.
What will I do?
Hmmm, let's see now . . .
My nephew ate it?
The dog scribbled on it?
My great Aunt Edna passed away.
Her funeral took up all day.
I was temporarily insane?
In a crash on a jet plane?
She's never going to buy those lines.
I better have a few more tries.
I was caught out in a big brush fire?
Chased by a mob killer-for-hire?
Shot at by a blind deer hunter?
Hit on the head with lightning and thunder?
"Pass them up, " the teacher said.
A million words passed through my head.
Here it goes: my brilliant plan.
I take the plunge and raise my hand.
"I forgot it!"

*David Au*

# UNTITLED

I was born yesterday on a CTA bus.

I'm not wearing
clean underwear.

I drink Pepsi.

I survived a 12-story
suicide jump.

I collect cigarette butts.

I think Clinton is a good president.

I recently disassembled
my Jaguar.

*Manoella Gonzalez*

# BULEMIC PANTOUM

I was tossing my cookies the other day

As the river flowed from my mouth I saw all the colors of the world

Little green men in shiny kayaks were paddling against the surf

And I squeezed my eyes convulsively

As the river flowed from my mouth I saw all the colors of the world

Splashing and dancing against the sterile porcelain like clumsy broken
chickens

And I squeezed my eyes convulsively

Because my weakness made me faint

Splashing and dancing against the sterile porcelain like clumsy broken
chickens

My contents fled from me

Because my weakness made me faint

I was tossing my cookies the other day

*Marquecia Jordan*

# . . .Who Swallowed a Fly

Erika choked when she felt something zip into her throat and lodge itself in there. She coughed a few times to try to dislodge it, but in an attempt to catch her breath, swallowed it instead. Dammit. What the hell was that anyway? She had just stepped out onto the balcony for a morning stretch, but was cut off in mid-yawn when something flew into her throat. A bug, perhaps? Maybe it was a fly. Oh well, whatever it was it would be swished around in stomach acid and digested like a piece of chicken. Not even a decomposing bug carcass to show for it. But what if it didn't die instantly? What if it still buzzed around inside her? The more Erika thought about it the more queasy she became. She found swallowing a bug almost as disgusting as seeing a rotten T-bone that had been festering in the boiling sun for a week, and crawling with so many maggots that it looked like steak and rice. She shook the image out of her head, because nausea had seized her appetite, killing the possibility of ingesting any kind of food for the rest of the day. Erika proceeded quickly to the bathroom for a drink of water. She picked up an empty plastic cup from the side of the black marble sink and placed it under the faucet. She turned on the water and watched it splash refreshingly into the cup. She gulped it slowly, savoring its cool taste as it filled the back of her throat and streamed down her esophagus. She belched loudly and patted her stomach boastfully. "Yep, that ought to take care of theat pesky fly. Drowning it should take care of it for sure."

The more she tried to believe that the fly didn't survive, the less Erika believed it. As the day passed, she had been plagued with severe nausea and the feeling of the insect still flying around inside her. She could feel it tickling the walls of her abdomen, cleverly avoiding being eaten by its gastric juices. She tried lying down and massaging her stomach, hoping a wave of acid would drown the little bugger once and for all. But, even lying down she could still feel it buzzing about. Her queasiness became unbearable. She wanted to throw up. She went back into the bathroom and knelt in front of the toilet. She pulled her braids off of her face and stuck her middle finger down her throat. She gagged at first, but then felt the vomit gush out of her mouth and nose and into the water, spattering onto her face. She vomited a couple more times, and then stood up at the sink, turning on the cold water. She splashed some on her face and looked up into the mirror at her dripping reflection, waiting silently for a sign. Thirty seconds passed. No buzzing. No tickling. Two minutes. Three. Erika had become sure that the fly had been puked up and is floating lifelessly in some sewer. She went into her bedroom to lie down and fell asleep almost instantly.

Erika was awakened half an hour later by that sickening fluttering in her stomach. "Jesus H. Christ!" She thought she had gotten rid of it. She sat up on the edge of her bed and clasped her hands around her face.

"Okay, Erika, you losin' it girl. It's all just in your mind . . . you do not have a fly buzzin' around your stomach. Remember, mind over matter, mind over matter, mind over matter . . ."

She tried to relax, lie down, watch a little T.V. She clicked on the television to a "Three's Company" rerun, the one where Jack, Janet and Terri mistake their neighbor's ventriloquist's dummy for a dismembered body. Even though she laughed falsely at their antics to forget about the fly, she couldn't. She still squirmed. She still felt nauseous. She still felt life inside her.

What was Erika gonna do? She felt her mind racing, folding itself over and under, inside and out, becoming a clump of useless, mashed gray matter. Call the hospital. No, that's crazy. She could hear them laughing and singing that crazy song: "There was an old lady who swallowed a fly/I don't know why she swallowed a fly/ perhaps she'll die." No, she won't die, she's just imagining things. "That crazy lady, perhaps she'll die" those hospital people would say. No. Not Erika. Not Erika Prince. She's not crazy, no siree, she won't die.

Erika wandered into the kitchen and spotted a bottle of Old Grandad on top of the refrigerator. It was usually reserved for bad colds and sweating out fevers, but today it would kill that fly. Kill the fly. She grabbed the bottle around its neck, twisted the cap off frantically, and turned it straight up. She took five swallows. The whiskey set fire to her chest and stomach. Whewwww, hot, hot, hot! That fly should be burnin' up by now.

She wouldn't wait to feel the fluttering, Erika drank furiously, till the liquor trickled down her chin and dripped onto her bathrobe. She drank until she was sprawled on the ivory linoleum , pissy drunk. She still clung to the empty bottle with one hand.

"Heh, hehhh . . . if that gotdammm fly ain't dead now, he shure is drunk as hell," she laughed through slurred speech. "Yep, too drunk to muuuve around."

Kind of like the way she was now.

"Take dat you stoopid bug! . . . didn't shpect this heyah booze ta be tha enda ya, didya?" She held up the bottle in reverence then dropped it to the floor. She tried, unsuccessfully at first, to pull herself up onto the kitchen counter, but finally managed to hold herself up. The liquor sloshed around her stomach, giving rise to another spell of nausea. She tried to stagger away, holding onto the counter, but fell on her butt instead. She propped up against the refrigerator.

She began to sing. "Dere wuzan ol' . . . crazy lady . . . who shwallowed a . . . fly . . . I dunno why . . . why she shwallowed a fly . . . maybe cuz she was hungry, heh heh heeehhh . . . maybee she'ull die . . . yeah, she'ull die . . . yep, kick dat bucket . . . maybee she'ull shwallow a spider ta catch that fly, heh hehh . . . "

Just then, Erika felt a stirring in her stomach. "No, Please God, no." She felt that same tickling that same ANNOYING, SICKENING, NAUSEAT-ING TICKLING!

"Oh God, help me . . . "she cried. "Why is this happenun' ta me?! . . . Wait—" She bolted upright and her face was mashed by surprise." —I kin heeyah yuh buzzin'! Just buzzin' — bzzz, dzzz, BZZZZ!"

Erika jumped up from the floor and tottered around the kitchen babbling to herself. "Oh God, I can't take diz . . . i'm gonna die! I'M GONNA DIIIEEE!"

She fell to her knees and wailed noisily. Her eyes lowered to the empty liquor bottle before her. The bottle. Yeah, she could use it to finally swat that fly. Cut off its pathetic little wings and watch its guts ooze from its dying body. She wrapped her hand around its neck and struck it against the floor. Shards of glass showered her face like a tumultuous rain.

Nick Avery had heard the screams penetrate the walls of his bedroom. He stood outside Erika's apartment banging on the door. He waited. No answer. He called her name, banged again. No answer. He walked down the hall to the office of Kenny, the building custodian, to get the keys. They returned to open Erika's door. Nick still knocked and called while Kenny fumbled with the key to open it. Once inside, Nick inspected the living room and bedroom while Kenny searched the bathroom and kitchen. Nick still called her name. Erika?!" Still no answer. He then heard a gasp from the kitchen, a faint "Oh my God." Nick hurried into the kitchen, where he saw Erika's body sitting in a pool of blood, her stomach ripped open, with the neck of a broken bottle sticking out of her.

*"There was an old lady who swallowed a fly . . . I don't know why she swallowed a fly . . . perhaps she'll die . . . "*

*Abra Johnson*

# AND I'M NOT TALKING ABOUT ROBERT FROST

Now he lays me down to sleep
Forever that horn Miles will keep
A smile on my lucid face
As Mr. Sandman tap dances on heavy eyes
To the tune of lingering Coltrane lullabies
Fused by Miles' cues
Construed kind of
Blue
In lieu
Of
Sad
Sad
Dreams
Stitched in quartered seams
Memorized in jazzy themes
Mesmerized
As I
Itch for more,
Scratchin' even in
R.E. M.
I CAN HARDLY REST IN WANT OF HIM,
MIIIIILESSSS.................................................
To go before I

ssssleeepp

I want.....
Miles to go before I sleep.

*Salvador Ortiz*

# THE SKETCHING SESSION

*John Newborne, a young professional fashion photographer, is confronted in his studio by a stranger, a middle-aged woman named Margaret Smith, on a rainy evening. John is strangely drawn to the woman and her tragic story of a broken marriage and a husband who abuses her. He unwittingly reveals his own dark past, much of which Margaret already knows. She makes an odd request — that John draw her, instead of shooting her photograph. John, troubled and motivated by forces he does not understand, agrees, and an eerie relationship begins.*

MARGARET: John?

JOHN: Yeah?

MARGARET: Won't you draw my portrait? You said you only worked with cameras. I know that's not true now. You're not a photographer. Maybe you feel it's not something you can bring back, but look at it this way.(JOHN stands and faces her.) Those recent sketches prove you never gave it all up.

JOHN: Margaret, I would love to draw you.

(MARGARET hugs JOHN. They walk out of the darkroom and into the bedroom area. MARGARET sees the telephone.)

MARGARET: Wait.

JOHN: Yes?

MARGARET: The rain might have cooled things off outside. Could you open the windows? Maybe that will make it better in here.

JOHN: That's a good idea. I'll get to it.

(JOHN exits and begins to uncover the large windows, Light streams in. During this time, MARGARET goes over to the phone. She dials a number and begins to speak low enough so JOHN won't hear her)

MARGARET: Hello? My name is Mrs. Margaret Smith. I'm from Norton, Massachusetts. Perhaps you may be looking for me. (pause) Yes. (pause) I am here in New York. You can find me at the following address: Thirty-four East Barrington Street. It's a large apartment complex, I am on the twenty-third floor, apartment number 238—the John Newborne Studios. Yes. I will remain here until then.

(MARGARET hangs up the phone, She walks out of the bedroom slowly and is pleased by what she sees.)

MARGARET: What a difference! What an absolute difference!

JOHN: (enthusiastically) Yes, yes. It's nice isn't it?

MARGARET: Marvelous! The rain did cool things off. Everything's fresh and renewed. I sure hope it did some good for those farmers' crops. I'm sure they'd welcome the relief with open arms. Such a wonderful breeze! (MARGARET spreads her arms into the air and lightly spins herself across the windows into John's arms.) Oh!

JOHN: (smiling gently) Easy now.

MARGARET: John?

JOHN: Yeah?

MARGARET: I just want to say how thankful I am that you've decided to draw me. Many times I've gone without the moments I long to enjoy.

JOHN: I'm glad this will be one you will enjoy.

MARGARET: Oh yes! And the first in a long time. Thank you.

JOHN: You're welcome.

(MARGARET walks over to the open windows and leans out to look at the Statue of Liberty, now visible.)

MARGARET: What a lovely view.

(JOHN joins her and also leans out.)

JOHN: See the statue?

MARGARET: How could I miss it?

JOHN: She looks especially beautiful at this time of day. And when the sun rises too. Did you ever think how wonderful it would be if we could have moments like this without having to worry about all that goes in between.

MARGARET: Well . . . I think unexpected rarity is what brings out the specialness in things. That can be just enough to provide the spirit with the desire to live on for the hope of these sacred moments.

JOHN: I see what you mean.

(JOHN crosses back to the studio area and sets up a chair in front of the subject's seat. He brings a large piece of thick white paper, a panel, and his pencils from the darkroom, and sits in the chair.)

JOHN: Whenever you're ready Margaret.

(MARGARET turns around and sees the setup.)

MARGARET: Oh? Here? (JOHN nods.) But you're not using the light, John. Look at all the wonderful light.

MARGARET: (walks over to the dividing curtain, draws it open, and a brilliant golden light fills the bedroom area.) My goodness! It's so much better here, John. (She sits on the bed.) This light can do so much for the portrait. After all, it's natural, unlike those funny lights that give off the same effect continuously. Besides, I think it just adds to the mood. (JOHN brings himself and his supplies over to the bedroom area. He puts them down and goes into the darkroom. He comes out with the stool, and he sets himself up on that.)

JOHN: Well, I'm all ready. Are you?

MARGARET: Yes.

JOHN: Now, how do you want this portrait of yours done?

MARGARET: Any way you like, John. I'll pose. The rest is all up to you.

JOHN: All right.

(MARGARET poses. JOHN begins to draw her with close attention.)

MARGARET: (suddenly, with concern) John?

JOHN. (looking up) Yes, Margaret?

MARGARET: There is something I have to tell you.

JOHN: (drawing) What is it, Margaret?

MARGARET: My reasons for coming here are not clear enough to you. And keeping them from you would also keep this portrait from having the meaning that I want it to have. This portrait is going to be more than just an image of myself, for it will have a history and a reason. But most importantly, there is a strong feeling about its meaning to me.

JOHN: What do you mean?

MARGARET: My husband did not leave me. I left him. (pause) About a week and a half ago, we were planning a day at the park with some of his friends. I started the day out with a hope that at least there would be some kind of peace waiting for me. (pause) Before we left, Andrew was packing the grill and the things we needed for the day at the park. I was inside the house, upstairs changing. When I finished, I came down and there was Andrew, waiting at the bottom of the stairs for me. "You're not wearing that," he said. I tried to change the subject, but still he persisted. "You are not wearing that," he repeated. "Why not?" I asked as I began to feel my heart beating harder and harder. "Because you don't look good in it," he replied, "and no matter how you look in that dress, that's nobody's business but your husband's, Now go upstairs and change." "No," I said. In a second, he was on me, pulling me by my hair as he tried to drag me up the stairs. Andrew hit me across my back with his powerful arms and kicked me. It seemed forever until I would reach the top of the stairs. But as I was slowly and painfully making my way to the second floor and he continued to beat me, a strange thing occurred to me. Every step up was a challenge to do something, to finally break out. But, I finally made it to the top. And when I went inside the bedroom to change, he stood near the door watching. (pause) After that, we got in his truck and drove to the butcher shop to pick up the meat we were taking for the barbecue. On the way there, he continued to scold me as if he was my angry father and I was nothing more than his rebellious daughter. But I didn't bother to argue with him. When we got there, he parked and went into the store for the meat, leaving me in the truck. My heart was still pounding hard and fast. I got out of the truck and went inside the butcher shop. He was in the back storage room. I went back there, but he didn't see me or hear me. Andrew was inside the freezer. I ran up to that freezer and shut the six foot high, cold, metal door with a noise that still lives in my head.

(JOHN has stopped drawing by now. He gets up from his chair.)

I bolted out the door, and ran outside of the room. Andrew had left the keys on the counter, so I locked up the place, got in the truck and drove away. And the strangest thing was that by the time I got back to the house, my heart was not pounding like it was before. Instead, a strange calmness had settled over me. Fifteen minutes later, I had a small suitcase with me and two thousand dollars in my purse. But before I left that house, I changed back into the other dress. (MARGARET gets up and shows off the dress she is presently wearing.) What do you think?

(JOHN walks out of out bedroom area astounded. MARGARET follows him.)

MARGARET: Do you want to know why the portrait I asked you to draw means so much to me?

JOHN: (nervously) I—I don't know about that. Maybe—-

MARGARET. (softly) Please, John, Listen to me, What I did was the one thing I could do at the time. And now I'm going to be a murderer in the eyes of the world, when in fact, I feel a survivor. And, I'm hoping to feel this way as time goes by. I'd like that portrait to be a manifestation of that. My image, produced by another person, will be a reminder of my attitude about myself now that I did something to recognize my own self-worth. But it will also give me a perhaps even more important thing. That portrait would be a connection with another person. You, John. Through this I will have established myself in front of another and even accepted as something real and full of life. Everyone needs to go beyond themselves and into someone else sometime in their life.

JOHN: (emotionally) You don't have to explain anymore. I understand.

(JOHN goes back to his seat)

MARGARET: Are you still going to draw me?

(JOHN begins drawing again and continues for not much longer,)

JOHN: It's finished.

MARGARET: (breaking her pose) Really?

JOHN. Yes.

(MARGARET rushes over to JOHN and takes a look. She is greatly pleased.)

MARGARET: (in awe) How did you ever do that?

JOHN: (smiling) The perfect combination of a great talent and a great subject. I mean that.

MARGARET: Why, thank you. And yes, you are a great talent. This is what's in you, John. Keep it going strong. Don't let it go to waste. (seriously) Thank you once again for doing this.

JOHN: My pleasure.

MARGARET: I will always cherish this portrait for it is a reminder of a small but meaningful moment, captured through the peace between two people.

(There is a knock at the door. JOHN and MARGARET are startled.)

MARGARET: They're here.

JOHN: Who?

MARGARET: Answer the door, John.

(JOHN remains seated, holding the portrait.)

MARGARET: Please, they are here for me. Just answer the door.

(There is a louder knock at the door followed by a voice saying: "Open up."
JOHN gets up and places the portrait on the chair, facing the audience. He
slowly crosses over to the hallway. MARGARET walks out of the bedroom
area and closes the curtain behind her. She crosses over to the studio and sits
in the subject's posing seat. JOHN opens the door and there are two policemen standing behind it.)

JOHN: Um, yes?

(During this time as JOHN talks to the cops, MARGARET gets up, crosses
upstage to the pictures between the windows, and begins taking them down
one by one, beginning with the one far stage left, opposite the real model
one.)

PARKER: Sir, I'm Lieutenant Parker, and this is Lieutenant Williams.
(Both show their badges.)We're from the New York Metropolitan Police
Department.

WILLIAMS: We received a call from this apartment by a Mrs.Margaret
Smith. Is she here?

JOHN: She's here to have her portrait done. What's the problem?

PARKER: Mrs. Smith has turned herself in for the murder of her husband
Andrew Smith. May we come in?

JOHN: Yes.

(MARGARET is almost finished taking down the pictures and placing them on the windowsills. When she finishes, the only one she leaves hanging is the picture of the real model, taken by Nathan. MARGARET crosses back to the studio and sits back down. The two cops enter.)

WILLIAMS: It's an out of state crime. Happened ten days ago in Massachusetts.

MARGARET: Mr. Newborne?

PARKER: Is that her?

JOHN: Yes, that's Mrs. Smith. Please, this way.

(JOHN leads the two policemen into the studio area where MARGARET is seated.)

PARKER: (to MARGARET) Are you the Mrs. Smith who called us?

MARGARET: Yes, I'm the one.

PARKER: Mrs. Smith, you're under arrest.

(The two policemen begin to arrest her and continue to read her her rights. JOHN only watches silently as they finish up.)

WILLIAMS: Thank you, Mr. Newborne. Be thankful you didn't get yourself involved any further.

(The two policemen begin to escort MARGARET out. JOHN runs into the bedroom area and comes out with the portrait. The cops and MARGARET' are about to reach the door.)

JOHN: Wait.

(The policemen turn around with MARGARET facing JOHN for the last time.)

PARKER: Yes?

(JOHN walks over to MARGARET with the portrait. He takes out a pencil from his pocket and signs the drawing.)

JOHN: This is yours, Margaret.

(WILLIAMS takes the portrait from JOHN.)

MARGARET: Thank you, John

(PARKER takes MARGARET out the door, WILLIAMS carries the portrait behind them and exits, closing the door behind him. There is a long pause before JOHN walks back into the studio. He notices the pictures missing from the wall and walks up to the windows. He sees the only picture up there of the real model and takes it down too. JOHN sighs, places it on the window sill along with the rest and slowly looks all around him in his apartment. Curtain falls.)

A mermaid is Death;
enchanting from a distant shore:
yet when her abyss is neared, she unveils her vanity,
and offers a revolting odor.

**ANTHONY ANTONIADIS**

# GALLERY 37 STUDENTS AND FACULTY

LITERARY COORDINATOR
Tanya Baxter

*Guild Complex*
*Creative Writing*

APPRENTICE ARTISTS
Natasha Binion
Victoria Cammon
Jennifer R. Clary
Audrey Conley
Felix Flauta
Manoella Gonzalez
Kambi Iverson
Farideh Karadsheh
Susan M. Kurek
Jivon Mackey
Melissa J. Molitoris
Jason T. Montemayor
Angela Pena
Jessica Savolainen
Zeeshan Shah
Nina L. Washington
Yoni D. Zeigler

SENIOR APPRENTICE
ARTISTS
Abra M. Johnson
Brendan Mattson
Sylvia M. Pyrich

TEACHING ASSISTANT
Judith Greer

TEACHING ARTISTS
Quraysh Ali
Glenda Baker
Emily Hooper

*Pegasus Players*
*Play Writing*

APPRENTICE ARTISTS
Chris C. Aleman
Danielle M. Cantrell
Tenika Frank
James Freeman-Hargis
Gina Holechko
Tiffany T. Hyler
Nia E. Lawrence
Benjamin J. Lieber
Yolanda T. Mitchell
Salvador Ortiz
Edward John Peterson
Juan-Jose Pichardo
Jasmine Santiago
Emily G. Schafer
Casandra Tukes

SENIOR APPRENTICE
ARTIST
Veronica V. Sansing

TEACHING ASSISTANT
Felicia Bradley

TEACHING ARTISTS
Eugene Baldwin
Marvin McAllister

*Young Chicago Authors*
*Creative Writing*

APPRENTICE ARTISTS
Anthony Antoniadis
David Au
Katherine Bardales
Adam Douglas Berry
Cristalle E. Bowen
Edith E. Bucio
Roberto Cardenas
Maisha Crawford
Jeff Daitsman
Maisha A. Fishburne
Delilah M. Garcia
Alicia Gonzalez
Roxanne Henry
Marlena R. Irizarry
Dan N. LaVorini
Melody R. Martin
Lekeishia S. McGee
Candice A. Murphy
Karl Osis
Rebecca Rodriguez
Adrienne Samuels
Ayanna M. Saulsberry
ChiHang-Michael Sit
Joaquin Soler
Katie A. Solka
Martha Villegas
Stephanie M. Wheeler
Sophia L. White
Aaron Williams
Boyle Wong

SENOIR APPRENITICE
ARTIST
Marquecia L. Jordan

TEACHING ASSISTANT
Jeanette Green

TEACHING ARTISTS
Chris Carstens
Nick Eliopulos
Yvie Raij